SWEET, LIKE RINKY-DINK

Mark Waldron was born in New York in 1960 and grew up in London. He works in advertising and lives in East London with his wife and son. He began writing poetry in his early 40s. He has published two collections with Salt, *The Brand New Dark* (2008) and *The Itchy Sea* (2011), and two with Bloodaxe, *Meanwhile, Trees* (2016) and *Sweet, like Rinky-Dink* (2019).

MARK WALDRON

Sweet, like Rinky-Dink

BLOODAXE BOOKS

ISBN: 978 1 78037 459 8

First published 2019 by
Bloodaxe Books Ltd,
Eastburn,
South Park,
Hexham,
Northumberland NE46 1BS.

www.bloodaxebooks.com
For further information about Bloodaxe titles
please visit our website and join our mailing list
or write to the above address for a catalogue

Supported using public funding by
**ARTS COUNCIL
ENGLAND**

Cover design: Neil Astley & Pamela Robertson-Pearce.

Printed in Great Britain by Bell & Bain Limited, Glasgow, Scotland, on
acid-free paper sourced from mills with FSC chain of custody certification.

For Marcie

ACKNOWLEDGEMENTS

Poems included in this book have appeared in *Bear Review*, *Long Poem magazine*, *Morning Star*, *Poetry*, *Poetry London*, *The Poetry Review*, *Poetry International* and *Tin House*. An earlier version of 'The body is a kind of home,' was written for English PEN in tribute to Zhu Yufu, a poet and political dissident imprisoned in China. A section of 'Sarouk Muhajeran' was written as part of an exchange of poems with Rebecca Perry.

I'd like to thank my friends Roddy Lumsden, Ahren Warner, Wayne Holloway-Smith and Ian Cartland for their comments and advice on these poems. I'd also like to thank my son Caspar Waldron for his helpful observations, and most of all my wife Julie Hill for her invaluable insights.

I'm grateful to Arts Council England for their financial support in the writing of this book.

CONTENTS

Wherever you drill into the world you'll find
its richness, dum-de-dee *(sic)*

ROBERT MANNING

I wish I loved lawnmowers

I really do wish I did. Because if I loved
lawnmowers I could go

to the lawnmower museum I just heard
about on the radio in a piece

about small museums.
It's in Southport apparently –

a seaside town *fringed to the north by
the Ribble Estuary*, according to Wikipedia.

It would be quite a trip to go up there,
and I'd almost certainly

have to stay the night. I think I might stay
in the Prince of Wales Hotel which looks

conveniently situated for the station
and the museum too. I can hardly bear

to think how much I'd be looking forward
to making that trip if I loved lawnmowers.

On the radio they said they have all sorts
of models from Victorian ones all the way

through to a state-of-the-art robot one
that's powered by solar energy.

If I was planning the visit I'd probably
have a bit of a virtual walk-round

on Street View, and in fact I've just done
exactly that in an effort to capture the feeling

I'd have if I was actually anticipating
a trip to the lawnmower museum.

Exploring the area I discovered
that Southport looks very much like

Weston-Super-Mare, where, as it happens,
I stayed in a halfway-house many

years ago, after doing a stint in rehab.
Now heroin – that I loved.

Brute Creation

Such vile humans are the animals, with their
gurning faces across which coverings of fur or scales
or feathers have spread like diseases of the skin.

How horribly deformed are their wretched bodies.
So many are born as freaks with legs where arms
should be; others emerge from inscrutable eggs

with flippers or fins or wings, or gills; or, as with
tortoises and crabs, they find themselves encased in
shells for pity's sake! Worms, in common with almost

every animal, have no hands, we know that; they
don't have one on each side. But it's what they have
instead that's their abomination, they have in place

of hands an absence of them, two shuddersome
profanities at which we cannot help but stare.
Horses also have no hands, they have their

clumping hooves instead, colossal single fingernails
which seem so brazenly to advertise a hopeless inability
to type or play piano (with any virtuosity at least).

Yes, how appalling is creation, how choc-a-block
with mockery! What an outrageous, miscreated
near-approximation of the human sexual organ

is the equine or the canine or the simian example;
as though each meant in its blasphemous familiarity
to drag us, and all our wives and friends and neighbours,

back down into the murderous, pitiless muck, where
we might slosh and fornicate and bark and squawk
and yell, blind once more to all the marvellous dirt.

Sixteen Found Dogs

As my friend Meredith used to say
before she got bit,

The grass is a dog in green costume, praying for release.
(Her words, not mine.)

Each of Meredith's words is a dog –
you'd agree if you knew Meredith.

So that makes twelve dogs so far.

Three stones thrown at a fence go *Arf, Arf, Arf* –
that's another three right there.

The ground is the last dog – if you throw
that dog a stick it will catch it every time.

Having pulled the stick down
to its enormous mouth

it will wait patiently
for you to throw the stick again. It will never tire.

The Take-Off

and bounces once,
then rolls till stopped

by the chock of its nose,
it rocks and comes to rest.
Straw in close-up,
the prickle of it against
the cheek, and then

she's up. Up and away,
Anne Boleyn balloon,
free now, tether cut, a baby
from its body born, rises,
hangs by a hundred thousand

strings of hair, and there's
just time to see the ground
and the body of the mum
who birthed her,
a fallen, riderless horse.

Las Aves Vacías

All the new birds
are made of nothing.

They have nothing inside
(for anti-ballast)

and those insides
are surrounded

in an outside nothing
which has its own

flibberti hole.
The birds,

they're nothinging
up there

in the nothing trees,
or on nothing roofs

under a nothing sky.
They fly of course,

but what is flying
if not nothing?

Sarouk Mohajeran

Did you not know it was me,
when you knelt down to pick up
your glove, that it was me
in the bristly touch of the carpet?

I'd had a suit made-up in its pattern
by finicky Persians, and then
I lay there for sixteen days wishing
you'd walk on me, hoping and praying

you'd lean down and touch me.
And then later – that knot in the wood
on the kitchen counter
when you were chopping the basil

and anchovies and capers
for the salsa verde, that knot
which looked just a little like my face –
it was my face, my darling!

That was me dressed-up as a plank.
I watched you look down at me,
your nose almost touched me,
I feared you'd hear the sap as it rose

so hotly beneath my woody veneer,
but your husband with his
bumpkin instinct intuited danger
and he called you away.

And then the me-like scent
you noticed in your drawing room,
well that was me too,
disguised as the harpsichord,

surely you knew! Surely you noticed
me stifle a sneeze when you tickled
my ivories so nicely, you maestro,
you impossible tease!

And when you sat by the river
to eat your Viennese pastry, that river
whose name you don't know –
well its name is my name, my angel!

It was me flowed helplessly
past you! Me, all riddled with quick
little fish and the big ones who
swallow them whole.

And the coconut shy at the fair,
surely you knew it was…
Ouch, that hurt! And then
the following week at the funeral,

the pale wood coffin,
you must have sensed it was
me from how well I wore it,
and the smoke which then rose

from the dispiriting chimney,
that furious plume whose thickening
billows so startled the birds who
know nothing of all our madness.

Your Face

Take a seat,
here in the kitchen.

Put your elbows
on the table

and your face
in your hands.

Now stay there
a moment.

That face
you can feel

as it rests against
your palms,

that face whose
hairline

is reached
by your fingertips,

whose ears
are touched

by your thumbs –
That's my face.

Diving for Pearls

The first thing which needs to be said is you should try to avoid a street fight at all costs because you might get hurt or arrested or even sued by your adversary or his family. But if you absolutely can't avoid one, then make sure to go all-out without the slightest hesitation with the most savage fusillade of blows. For heaven's sake don't try to act as though you're some kind of professional, or as though you're in a movie or something, and throw stylish punches between neat little dance steps; no, you just need to reach quickly, as quickly as you possibly can, into that part of your enemy, that part which exists in every beast, which will always hanker to back-off. You have to furiously search for that place as though you had taken a gasp of air and then plunged under and were swimming down to the deep seabed to scrabble among the murky rocks for a silver key which unlocks the way back to the surface. You need to reach that sweet spot with a flurry of hard punches and kicks and determinedly vicious grabs to the balls and scratches and all-out bites and gouges to the eyes, and hair yanks and spit in the face. Your opponent will surely say to themselves: *This person is a madman who knows no restraint, it's okay and not cowardly at all to run away from a madman*, and they'll bolt off, ducking into the woods. They'll say to their wife later as she dabs their cuts with rags, *I'd have beaten him good if he hadn't been a madman*, but they'll be frightened that even if she doesn't yet know it, it's you she'll want now, and she will.

Sweet, like Rinky-Dink

My sweet me is not like an igloo, not like a canoe
or a crocodile. No, she's like a canoodle.

I love her so much, she is ding-dong-dishy, she is a song,
a song-ditty you can lick to the tip of.

I kiss her in a way that alludes to kissing.
I hug her in a way that refers to hugging.

I bite her in a way that references biting.
We fandangle in a way that connotes fandangling and so on.

Good heavens, we allude in a way that alludes to alluding,
but I suck my me as a leech might –

to get me off you'll have to burn me with cigars.
You'll have to lop my head off.

The Stick

Existence trumps non-existence every time. It has
all the colours and all the shapes and all the moves,

it is rude in its bounty and its grotesque reach which
overcomes all before it. This bit of stick I found in

the park was showing off because the dead can't have it.
They can't have any of it. It was sticky and prickled

with a showy, dazzling presence, though it's quietened
a little now, now that I've taken it home

and have it here on the mantelpiece. It has dressed
in purple robes and carried its being like a chalice

with such disarming mock-solemnity down and down
the pale carved steps into its candlelit depths.

Its being rests inside it now and purrs quite inaudibly
with a sound like the most exclusive refrigerator,

or a sound you might take for your own sovereign
wheels spinning. Little stick. Wait for me. I'm coming.

Light that falls

upon its object, caresses
and warms it and whispers its name to thereby

excite it,
so that in that object's improper celebration

it might shriek and giggling shuck off
those sombre black mourning clothes

it dons each dusk, and so expose itself licentiously
to that returning light's eager ogle.

It might proffer all the shiny coloured
morsels it has, some of which shift

or quiver or undulate,
or shine with a gloss of fallen rain.

How quick, that light, it works to titillate
those surfaces it fondles,

to arouse them,
bring them up as truffles dug from earthy brooding,

or raise them as happy fish
trawled from the deep,

glinting and thrashing and visible at last to us,
the light's screaming followers.

WW1 Marcie

Professor Zeppelin is droning over Kent,
carpet-bombing Marcie to give us all

something creaky to rub up against.
Marcie catches his spherical bombs

(un-pocked despite eons of stiff kisses)
in her apron, which she holds out as though

she meant to collect pommes. She smiles up
at the professor as she catches glimpses

of him through the leaves,
and he looks smiling down on her like God.

Kent and the whole of England roll away
swooning dreamily, cocooned

in an intoxicating mist of honeybees and pollen
that's filtered through our timorous sensibility

to produce an even more intoxicating,
somewhat paler mist of a quite terrific potency.

Back in The Dog and Bone, Marcie racks-up
the round bombs which are all the germane elements

of her summer's morning, and cueing-up
on the green baize she then breaks emphatically,

which the bombs, of course, adore.
Clack clack-clack-clack-clack! She pots the lot,

rumble, rumble, clunk, rumble–rumble.
Marcie and her fuzzy friends look appalled

that the table should have scoffed everything.

What are things

if not what they seem?

Take a lemony bird.
Have it.

An up-down nestling tree,
a sudden impromptu rumba,

an old sky,
a bare wind. Have it and have it.

The sounding line,
its sleepy plummet.

The *boom*, *boom* of calling.
Have it.

The body is a kind of home,

flesh-bricked, skin-dipped, dirt-grouted,
scaffolded within by sticks,

its homely odours hang from it.
It is festooned in the visible,

and bucket-challenged with the selfhood
that splashes over it

and wakes it every moment gasping
from its dumb slumber.

Does a squandered blade blunt agin time's grit?
And what of it?

Does it lie in the drawer, I say, blunting
as glass drips?

I heard a story once, or I dreamt it:
A pilot downed over Manpo,

and held since then in solitary
confinement, had designed, to keep

his sanity, a castle in his mind, or so
he told a priest who once did visit him.

And though my circumstance
is somewhat less adverse, I do the same

at night when I find myself undoused
by dark but lit inside by wakefulness,

unable to shuck the day's husk,
its dusty glamour,

its still reverberating clamour.
I have built a home within imagination's

flyblown realm, which itself emanates
from the body's fertile kingdom.

My castle goes like this:
grown, for so it seems, on a tall

black rock just off the black shore
and built of that black stone,

it towers neath a black sky.
The castle has but one thin

connection to the coast –
a long drawbridge slung between

the gate and the headland's cliff.
Under assault from land,

and with the drawbridge raised,
besieged inhabitants can lower

wicker baskets down to friendly ships,
and from them lift supplies

of lemons and cake, piglets
and parsnips.

And should the sea be too rough,
or the enemy have mastery of it,

well then a tunnel has been chipped
from the island's stone.

A spiral stepped drop which reaches
through the twice-black rock,

down beneath the sea floor,
where levelling, it proceeds toward

the shore, before it gently climbs once
more, and, some mile or so inland,

beneath a skull-studded hatch it
surfaces among the cluttered bones

in the charnel house of a half-ruined
church. Roofless, the building's

structure offers no shelter to a shepherd
or besieging knight whose camp

may be near. And besides, the dead
sepulchred here within the vaults

would fill the least superstitious
with such dismay that they'd surely

retreat from its grim propinquity
should they reconnoitre it.

Forgive me, though,
for describing my elaborate

diversion. The castle and its environs,
their function is to distract only myself,

so that I might, as I tinker with some
detail of an architrave or arrow slit,

not perceive the pit, and so might
fall in it – that trap which soft-shod sleep

with muffled spade, each night
in some new and unexpected spot

has laid in hope that I, its willing
quarry, might, stepping back, be captured.

And my purpose in describing
my sanctuary within whose

refuge I have spent so many nights,
was not that I wished like some

vulgar salesman to draw your attention
to the assiduity I've lavished

on its construction, or to the variety
and opulence of its furnishings.

No, I brought you here because I felt
I must share a recurrent and troubling event:

I have on more than one occasion,
when glancing out the leaded window

of my favoured chamber, seen
a single candle lit in the other

tower which stands beyond the inner bailey.
A candle always at that moment

snuffed, as though my astonished
gasp had drawn away its succour as a gust.

Hobnobbing with Elephants

where *elephants* stand in
for *walnuts*

which in turn stand in
for something else wrinkly.

(Elephant babies I love u tho! xx)

Age is not made reference to
because of its cordiality with death –

see how they walk together
on the promenade sharing a single parasol –

also because the old aren't bouncy,
lacking give.

I don't miss you so much as miss you
something awful.

It's as though I lost my nuts
in the woods

and never re-found them
among the plethora of others.

And now dotage sidles up to me
and shows me my failings

as though sand blew off
a buried ruin.

Where are you baby-me? Still spinning
in my womb.

A Scabbarding

And so I sheathed my blade up to its hilt
inside the quick slot of its brand-new slit
(that hovel of a home, which, as a peasant
must, the knife did fabricate for its own self).
It slipped so neatly inter-twixt my sticks,
right through my unsuspecting bits and pipes.
So sharp was it, so subtly did it make
its way inside, and with such an easy charm
that my old-fashioned and courteous innards
seemed for a moment welcoming
to the cold and patriarchal feel of metal.

They appeared quite in awe of it, my sweet
provincial organs, until they came suddenly
upon their shock, and saw at last how the steel
had burst so boorishly into their inner sanctum.
Pathetically they tried then to cover up
their virgin modesty, grasping at all the nothing
that they had. And as the blade, without a smile,
with nothing but a cruel and cutting little nod
withdrew, they found that they were
alone again, and as they hurt and bled
they prayed successfully for its prompt return.

Manno

Robert Manning is having my cake
and eating it.

It's de-scrumptious
from the off.

Manning is wearing something haywire
in order to tickle me.

The Marcie cake on the plate
on the table is layered

with sponge and a stratum of Marzipan
and then more sponge, topped off

with a thin icing of lickable that's sprinkled
with hundreds and thousands

of different coloured kisses.
Every now and then Robert tots

his Marcy cake, but there is never
any of her eaten. He takes another slice

and noshes off that pointy end that comes
from a cake's middle,

that bit that's least cooked
and consequently

moistest, that portion
of a cake that's most furiously happy.

A Drip

When thrown, Manning flown more like an stone
than a aeroplone, as in: he flown down.

It's so temptish to have my way with Mannish,
because he's mine, the silly old clown, as in clone.

I get him on the telephine,
Hello Manning, I says. He says nothing.
As in he says: *No thing*.

What do you mean 'No thing', Manning? says I.
(What an proper cunt that Manning is considering he's me.)

Manning's flying his plone.
It's having the whole fat sky like an pig,
helping itself to lashings of it like somebody's business.

Forgive me, but I seem to have mislaid my cologne.
Oh, there it is, hiding under the telephine
like an bottle of vodka with an drip in it,

that last drip that you can't get out because it's so slow,
because it lingers so. Poor drip. Poor Manno.

Oh no,

Manning's only gone and gone down again.
There he is in his blue submarone,

no, aeroplone, no, bathroom, no, bed,
no, blue submarone.

Bless Manning, all underwater in his sunkenness.
What an special hell underwater is –

how dare everything
that goes on under there go on!

Manno says... Well I don't know what Manno says,
of course not no no I don't.
I can't come up with an proper nothing like an wisp might.

But wait! Is that Man I hear, who speakin' through
his blowhole hole says
he don't knowhow how he's summat like an fish, a oily one,

or something like born or something,
or something like made of plastico, or some other material,
one that's both living plus dead?

Oh sorry piece of meat or wood
or earth or cheese for goodness' sake!

What Manno says *emerges*,
he's just egged on by me to be summat.

Do you see the old goat a-buying a aeroplone?
Swapping it for lemons. An lorra lorra lemons.
What's that about? What's what's any of it properly about?

Coming Through!

Manning's flying his Boom Bang-a-Bang agin.
Parp! it goes at the yellow-belly sky,

and the sky scrambles out of the way.
Parp! Parp! and the sky gets out of the way.

Oh lummy, this is the life when one's flying
one's ticker like a aeroplone,
and the sky's jumping out of the way
Parp Parp! quick-sharp.

But Manno's plone's a old clown plone.
Its nuts come off, and them wings wiv 'em,
and them doors fall off,
and them tail an' wheels an' fuselage,

an' Man's bits – them drop off too,
his nuts, his toes, his fuselage.

There goes Manno's kissy-kissy lips,
them go down sans parachute.

His very moniker itself unmakes as though a-mockin'
his catastrophe.
There's only a apostrophe left hangin' in the air.

Endpiece

Only my winkle is de-facto,
and even it

isn't really, mutters Manno.
Though its jiggle

does surely purport
some quiddity,

he intones posthumously
as we kick

what's left of him
into the long grass.

Later,
at the awards ceremony,

I lean across to my neighbour.
Of course, I yakker,

he was nothing but
a cowboy in a blowhard sandwich

when it came right down to it,
which, I might add, it never did.

And we smile two mingy
little smiles.

Supination

It feels more effortless and natural
for the right hand

to turn a screw clockwise
than it does to turn it anticlock.

The screw's thread converts
a clockwise revolution

to a going in, as the screw impales
its first object

and then penetrates the next
to bring the two together.

We have made it easier to do
than to undo. We should be careful.

How to Get a Gibbet through the Small Hole

It ain't going sideways that's for sure. And truth be told, it probably ain't going lengthways either unless you really know what you're doing; plus if someone's hanging from the rope then you've got to factor that into your calculations before you even embark on the manoeuvre. The first thing to say is there's no point in working the gibbet itself through the aperture and then finding that the fragile cadaver firmly noosed on this end of the rope won't go through. In fact you'd be in real difficulties then as you won't extract the gibbet back *out* once you've got it through, because it'll just be hanging there any-old-how on the other side and you'll never get it properly aligned to come back again, so you'll have a stiff on this side of the hole, and a gibbet on the other side with the rope connecting them. What are you going to do then? Look round over your shoulder with a *Can anyone help?* raised eyebrows expression on your face? I think not. And I imagine, if you're honest, you probably think not too. No, I'd actually recommend starting with the corpse itself. Feed the body slowly through the hole, feet first obviously, and both feet mind – don't try getting one foot and leg through and then starting on the other one or you'll get in a frightful salmagundi and possibly break something. Then once you've given the dead patsy's head a last gentle push, and he's popped through and is safely dangling in the other bailiwick, out of harm's way, you can start on the gibbet itself, which is less susceptible to damage, so you can fiddle about with it with carefree abandon, and conceivably even begin to derive some modicum of pleasure out of the whole enterprise.

Poor light,

what a saint you are, shining on everything,
drawn to the world like flames are to moths,
like honey to bees. So readily do you dole
yourself out, and in such abundance so that
we might operate our otherwise redundant eyes.
For they'd be useless even as pretty bibelots
that studded the otherwise dull surfaces of faces.

No, in your absence, in that total darkness
the eyes wouldn't see or even be seen, and they
would soon shrivel up and desiccate, die out
from pointlessness just as the little toe will
(unless we can find a way to reverse its long
decline). Hey, plump eyes! Isn't it time you put
your tiny wet hands together for the light!

Angry with Trees

What shameless cheats
the trees are.

How poker-faced with
their unbeatable

hands of identical cards,
an uncountable flush

thrown down on the baize
with an obnoxious flourish

just as each card
with its oft-repeated green

turns red and brown
and yellow and orange,

and the trees gather up
their winnings by sucking

the poor ordinary ground as
they get ready to play again.

Well fuck you, trees.
I never met a blasted tree

that didn't have my taste
stuffed in its

wood mouth,
an ace in the hole.

The Dragonfly and Berries

Perhaps, like me, you live in a house with two
staircases. Well good for you if you do because they're
almost always the larger types of property, and so
living in one suggests you are probably fairly affluent.

Another reason it's propitious to live in habitations
with two staircases is the opportunities they provide
for the occupants to surprise each other.
For example, one person might wander off in front

of another, and then appear suddenly behind them
like an apparition and cause them to shriek
and throw the laundry all over the wolfhound,
or throw the dachshund all over the secretary.

One other good reason to live in a house with
two staircases is that you can spend time lying
in bed of a morning wondering which might be
the shortest route to go down to the dining room

for the kippers, and perhaps you'll measure
the two options by pacing them out in fairy steps,
or if you're like me you might ask one of the interns
to do so on your behalf. But the best thing of all

is only to wait until people are out on errands or
holidays or visiting the neurologist, and then to run
round and round the house, up the backstairs,
across the landing with the faded fauteuil,

past the doors to the bedrooms, then down the front
stairs to the hallway, and through to the kitchen with
the half-plucked woodcock, and back up the backstairs,
across the landing with the faded fauteuil and the books

on the table, past the bedrooms, down the front stairs
to the hallway, and then through to the kitchen with
the half-plucked woodcock on the long pine table,
and back up the panelled backstairs,

across the landing with the faded fauteuil
and the books on the table and the Alcaraz rug,
past the doors to the bedrooms and down the front
stairs with the painting of the dragonfly and berries

to the hallway. And that's where you'd find me
talking to the aerial photograph interpreter,
except that it's me who's running, just look
at me go, how marvellously happy I am!

My Hopeless Marcie

she hasn't got her own special lips
or her own special arms.

Or scent, or skin.
Or face or bones.

Or hair,
or blood, or piss.

She thinks she can leave me
but she can't because

she hasn't got no legs either.
No, she's only got mine,

and they're right here under me
running,

running with Marcie, quickly away.

Ice Cream for I Scream

It's summer, and just the sunniest
of afternoons.

Outside the sanatorium,
in the arboretum, the attendees

are served their teas.
The strudel is toothsome

when Herr Stumpf, from the lectern,
contradicts the consensus

that I is for ice cream. No, now
he's proposing that I's for spaghetti,

all spaghetti, he avers,
being once alphabetti,

all spaghetti being once that capital I
that it is when it's dry,

not the maddening doodle that it is
when it's done and awry.

His audience listen,
but once he has spoken,

then beneath their applause
that's not fulsome but token,

they don't soften, no rather, they stiffen.

As Though Begat, but Not

My you-train
toy-real

all stocked
in her station

What am I like
State – state-away peppercorn

I'm mostly ears
a sudden god gone happy

This life of ours
it's grinding out poor dear old train

It's grinding out poor

How scrubbed-up clean

are our spirits, these loquacious silver gods who glide at
some safe distance above their rank and proletarian bodies.

Foul though fascinating landscapes they are that they
traverse, besmirched with armpits and fruity genitalia

and belching gobs and those impulsive blurting sphincters
in whose hot updrafts they might ascend and soar.

O, but our spirits are so lustrous, so hairless, so advanced
in their glass-bottomed flying machines which run on

just about nothing! What quick and icy notions they have
which slot into one another like the tightest clocks, and how

they lick their lips as they gaze down in anticipatory glee,
for though they would not themselves wish to rough it,

they certainly will peep through their bedroom
windows, each a jiggling voyeur of its own ardent body

when that body has chanced upon another, and the pair
of them have knuckled down to their immersive work.

The first time I came upon him,

the cockroach was stood upright upon his hindmost
legs, and leant insouciant against the bin, the one
they keep recycling in. He smoked a cigarette
and blew smoke rings so small and thin you'd think
that this galumphing world would not support 'em.

His behaviour seemed as that of some impossible
insect that might only breathe a cartoon's magic air,
or one that inhabits a dream maybe, or a vision, or
that he must be a fictive critter meant to serve the ends
of a fairy tale. But the way in which he reached

out his claw and flicked his ash upon the kitchen floor,
and the way that ash settled there and then twitched
in a draft like a tiny tumbleweed, left no room
to doubt that his existence was firmly lodged inside
the proper world. On seeing me, he extinguished

quick his cigarette upon his own stiff abdomen,
tossed the butt up into the air and catching it in
his mouth, swallowed it in one exaggerated gulp
and then looked at me with an expression which
would, I'm sure, had he a mouth capable of grinning,

or lids with which to blink, have been a cheeky smile
and a wink. As though compelled, I found that I
did hurry to the counter where I dislodged a minute
portion from a parmesan and which I then presented
to him. He took the cheese with a little bow

and pocketed it somewhere beneath his oily carapace,
presumably with the intention of consuming it
at some later date. I knew full well of course
that I was not mad to believe that what I witnessed
was quite palpable, quite actual, so when my friends

came round that afternoon to play our weekly game
of Polignac, I felt no surprise at all when they calmly
put away their wings, and with their compound eyes
like disco balls glinting, one by one did introduce
themselves so imperturbably to our newfound friend.

How to Tap a Field Mushroom

Don't, is the short answer. But do is shorter still. Have you ever tried to get up-wind of an authentic tombola? One that's really kicking off with music and LED lights, bright in the midday sun? Because that's the kind of hubba-hubba we're talking about here. Gloves is obviously one issue that springs to mind. Gloves or no gloves. Opinions vary. Back in the day no one would have dreamt of tapping a mushroom without wearing one glove minimum – on your left hand if the shroom's going anticlock, on your right hand if not. Nowadays opinion is divided over the question. The younger folk like to go completely barehanded as a kind of rite of passage, and a statement I suppose to us old-timers. I understand that, I was young once. But in the end surely it's not what works best for you, but what works best for the fungi. And though we can't ask them, we can surely get a sense of what's right according to the natural order of things, and whether an absence of glove might seem at all disrespectful, to the tradition if nothing else. It's something that only comes with time – the fully-fledged ability to really get down and attend to the babbling actuality. And that's how come I fall so firmly on the glove side of the fence. Sorry.

A Closed Sandwich

Underneath the wickedness

is something adorable and sorry.

And underneath that?
I'll kill you.

And under that,

a meadow,
spattered with boy-crazy wildflowers.

They hurt with what it is to be thought of.

The main event

was certainly the boy with a hundred and nine heads.
They were each in themselves quite minuscule,
no more than the size of a smallish olive,
and were all clustered, cheek by jowl, along the top
of the child's shoulders, as well as in the space
where a neck would normally be.
Up they stuck upon their tiny stalks, every one
with a sibling's similarity, for they each represented,
as the leaflet cumbersomely put it: ...*in miniature,*
a possible outcome for the appearance of a single head,
had the child possessed but one...

Some heads were handsome, some less so.
Some had wavy hair, some straight,
four or five wore spectacles so small one needed
glasses of one's own to see them,
some were better at maths than others, some,
we were told, excelled at history, some at science,
though overall there was a propensity towards
an aptitude for languages and music, as well as dance,
which we were to witness executed with the most
astonishing grace. An accomplishment which seems
all the more extraordinary when one considers
that each move had to be signed off, as it were,
by the great parliament of individual consciousnesses.

Or perhaps once those minds had come
to an agreement as from whence their body might
embark upon its improvised routine, then each
gesture fell inevitably out of its predecessor,
and engendered its successor as their shared frame
plunged forward or backward or spun
with a beast's abandon into its next arrangement,

toppling onwards and onwards
like a happy crowd into its shared ecstasy.

The dance commenced when our guide, their keeper,
took up his fiddle and began to play a jig upon it.
The tiny heads at once began to nod at first
autonomously, each with his unique rhythm,
but then by turns they fell into a happy
synchronicity, smiling and nodding this way
and then that, before their combined wills
seemed to coalesce about the fingers which began
to drum forcefully upon the desk at which
the body sat, and then quite suddenly
the whole figure rose from its chair sending it
clattering across the floor as the body burst
with a delicious fury into its rollick, the row
of heads seemed as screaming happy children
flung hither and thither on a fairground ride,
and we, the little group of visitors, I admit,
soon found ourselves clapping and stamping
and shouting without inhibition,
our encouragement. Once the dance had come
to its end and the flushed and panting little heads
had taken their bows while we their spellbound
audience applauded and whooped with delight,
then we retired to the keeper's private rooms
for to speak with him a while.

No punishments, he told us as he filled his pipe,
had ever been administered,
because since they shared a common stomach,
to deny supper to one would have meant denying
supper to all, and to punish one with a spank
administered to their common posterior
would of course have punished every one of them.

Indeed he said, he believed it was because
they knew they could not be singled out,
that they each elected to behave so well,
and never once chose to organise themselves
into a mob under the leadership of the most
hot-headed among them, and then to ignite
an insurrection in which they might chant
galvanising slogans protesting against
their confinement here, and induce
with their focussed wills their relatively enormous
fists and feet to punch and kick the doors,
let alone their keeper, or god forbid, ourselves,
the paying visitors who's interest helps to feed
the young rascals or should I say rascal!

But no, all-daylong, when not at their lessons,
they chattered and laughed, passed whispered
cheeky secrets down the line, told each other
stories, and sometimes sang the most beautiful
rounds in tiny voices which together produced
a sound with the volume one would expect
to issue from a normal child.
And all night long they slept alone in their room,
or so their keeper told us, as though
in the happiest dormitory it was possible to imagine.

No wonder

we're miserable, seeing as we don't know what's happening.
Plants tick,

and the neutered soup of dust dinders in-between,
sweet jester.

Harrumph and again

the earth offers up its rough parchment of hunger,
and insisting on it ad infinitum.

(No, I don't know either.)

Silly blown earth with its trivial
import and the tracks we left in it. I love your tracks btw,

that are so brim-full of emptiness. Where did you go exactly?

I have taken to following myself
because I'm imitable. I don't know what more to say.

A Flying Visit

Sweetheart and Hogarth (remember him?)
popped down on the long-lost overdub.

Sweetheart's Scaramouche ran everyone ragged,
and rightly so,

with its blues & greens and purples and yellows
and reds and oranges, and blues and greens again,

as though colour had only been invented last week,
and was still getting its ridiculous house in

order. Still, the flavour of peppercorns was
pervasive, and one thing lead

to another & then right back to the one thing again,
in a kind of delightful continental toing

and froing of the sort we used
to snort about, if that's still kosher. You tell me.

Ordinary People, We Just Don't See Them

If, in an experiment, you're made to spend some time sealed into a comfortable environment with a hundred and forty-nine astonishingly beautiful people, it will seem strange and unsettling at first, but you'll start to acclimatise to it soon enough. In fact it'll appear really quite normal after a week or so. And if, after another three weeks have gone by, you're sent back out into the ordinary world, then you'll find, from the moment you step out of the little side door onto the busy street, that the average people going about their business look worse than pigs and dogs and beetles and bashed aliens from a nasty dirty planet. They might wear clothes which they hope will make them more attractive but, in a cruel joke, the clothes will only serve to make matters worse, and they'll come across as nothing but hideous caricatures, as though they were almost beautiful people but had somehow gone skew-whiff catastrophically at the last moment, and spun off into monstrousness – no matter, it seems, that *ordinary* might be only a tweak on the dial, or one lobbed brick away from beauty.

The Wild West

Is one a hermit,
soft in a grotto?

Is one a lodger,
a squatter,

a worm in its apple?
You fill your body

so neatly to its brim,
and I've noticed how

your eyes are cleverly
aligned with its two

window holes,
so you can peer out

at the world beyond
your haunt,

and also so we can see
those eyes of yours,

holed-up in there,
desperate desperados

hatless in their hideout,
surrounded by

this posse
I've betrayed them to.

Will they ever
forgive me?

Even now that we live exclusively

inside, and take no joy in any pleasures of the world,
still we find we are compelled to eat,

for we are driven to it by hunger.
And still we find we are compelled to seek a private space

and a comfy surface. Yes, even though to copulate
is not what it once was,

is not, indeed, the slightest bit so lusciously exquisite,
we continue to take our skirts and trousers off,

and diligently prepare our bits by the application
of a little spit and polish by which

we might encourage numb thickenings to manifest
(such as when the ankles are exposed

to the increased temperatures of the Italian Riviera,
or when plant cells are made turgid

by the action of osmosis, and are able then to support
a non-woody stem).

Before those effects wear off, we get down to the task proper.
Grimacing, we achieve insertion,

and then, as we talk cookery or politics,
or, leaning to one side, stroke the cockatoo,

we enact those still-remembered motions with our loins,
those repetitive in-outs that must

eventually induce the male protuberance to blurt
its speech bubble,

just as an albatross's gullet,
when a chick stimulates that bird's bill,

will instinctively emit for it a meal of dumb soup.
The children which we thus produce,

they carry thin and hostile knives secreted in their boots.
We should be wary of them.

What are you doing taking the air

in the Blapetty Gardens little saint I can't tell you.
Birds thither.

Did the commissariat decree.

And you had toast, you say,
beneath beans for your breakfast at the Blapetty Palace.

Cranky guards, enamoured, armoured, peppered, peeped,
enamelled, clanky, chalky.

(I can't help it, I love you.)

Dear reader, unlikely bedfellow, I don't like you she implies.

My God, my Marcie's got

a lovely jubbly cock. I'd just adore it if I saw it,
if I smelt its cheeky scent,

and I would experience a jolt
so Christmassy when she showed it me,

resting on a Lincoln Green velvet cushion,
one hung with portly golden tassels.

I'd be infused indeed
with that happy sang-froid

one sometimes has in a dream,
and I would wonder if the whole world

weren't made this way,
and that I might reach down

beyond my belt's prim resistance,
to touch my pretty quim in its everted reverie.

My brain likes fish,

I read it a thing about
how fish is good for
brains, and now my
brain likes fish. I can't
even remember reading
it this thing about how
fish is good for it, but
anyhow, now it just goes
on and on and on and on
about how it likes fish
and how fish is good for
it, and how I should give
it it. I feel sorry for my
brain banged up in there
obsessing about this kind
of shit. It's ridiculous
and maybe a bit gross,
but I want to take it out
and give it a kiss. Is that
ok? And maybe I'd give it
a gentle squeeze too, not
a proper hard squeeze, I
wouldn't want it to sort
of squirt out of my grasp
and fly across the room
as though this were some
stupid screwball cartoon,
and maybe damage itself
on something, such as the
corner of the mantelpiece.
I can barely bring myself
to picture the look of
hurt reproach etched in
its surfaces.

My brain is a fool,

sitting in the plush lounge with the dim lighting,
it doesn't know what's happening.

It's an ingénue, a yokel, ordering drinks shyly,
eating peanuts, licking its fat fingers.

It's a Rubenesque shepherdess my brain, all adrift in
the big city, its sheep lost long ago.

Poor brain, you don't know who you are, whistling
the tunes you wrote for another age.

My dumb brain it can't even scrawl its own name on
the wall because the pen keeps falling out.

In order to stave off the dark my stupid brain is hiding
in an alleyway twiddling the labyrinthine

crevices that it has. My brain don't know if it's coming
or going. I know though: It's going.

My boneheaded brain

is relaxing by the pool drinking
Tia Maria for its zinc content.

My brain has slipped
out of its uncomfortable skull,

that has my scalp and hair on it,
popped that safely under the lounger,

and is lying on its front
on a hotel towel

taking it easy after
a hard morning's *fiddling* as my

brain puts it. It's lathered in factor
50 that a passing celebrity chef

has helpfully massaged into it
because it has no hands

or any other means
to do that for itself,

and it would certainly burn in no time
in the Canary Islands sun

without any protection
against the UV rays.

Down on the beach yesterday
my klutzy brain got

sand in its cracks, and
the celebrity chef just unexpectedly

fished some of it out as he
applied the sunscreen, working it deep

into the sulci.
It glistened on his fingertips

like a cluster of minuscule jewels,
and looking up from those

glinting constellations
he wondered for a moment

at the whole world's dreamt-up
system of values. My brain sensed

his wondering and smiled.
Have you ever seen a hot

brain smile beneath the noonday sun?
It's kind of cute.

The words you sweat,

they may dissemble.
But you find you cannot

mince your scent,
or choose it carefully,

for it secretes your secrets
with its abandoned openness,

and you can't take back
what's advertised by that

attendant animal, that consort
who rests beside you,

abandoned to its whim,
and breathes,

and licks its own face.
You can't smile,

or stretching, look away
to offset its implication

because it speaks as though
behind your back and makes

arrangements only
with others of its own kind.

The Lighthouse Keeper

On occasion, when the mood takes him
as it so often does, he will put down

his papers, get up from his kindly old chair,
and leave for a while the sweeping beam

to sow its charitable seed – that seed which,
when falling on the ground

of a helmsman's fertile consciousness,
ought germinate in it a cautious vigilance.

He descends then, the long corkscrew of
the stairs and opens at their base the metal door

so that he may take a closer look at what might
be beyond his tower's environs. There he always

finds the churning world, she laps at him from
every side with no respite, and spatters him

with spray. Thanks to a certain modulation,
a tone which he adopted long ago

when he still wore shorts and buckled shoes,
there is no danger here, from neither shark

nor crocodile, not in this sea stuffed as it is
like a dressing up box with whimsy.

Indeed, were there such creatures hidden
neath the sliver-thin surface of the waves,

they'd have no teeth but only soft grey gums
and goofy grins, and they'd be giggling

knowingly at the whole thing. And so it is
that as he gazes out, he cannot help

but wonder what it is he might be warning of
with the light which turns atop his tower,

because that tower is itself in fact the only
hazard anywhere on which a ship might rip her

wooden skin and haemorrhage her lumpy
blood that's made of all the gasping sailormen.

Buddies

Sometimes I have wished my dong
were an impossible leviathan

that protruded, with a person's girth
from my loins where we'd be

as conjoined twins conjoined.
It would rise to my head height,

so that I might, each morning
as I lay in bed, reach my arms around it,

hug it tight, pressed against my belly
and my chest, rest my cheek against

its helmet-sized helmet, and with my
eyes squeezed shut, hold it thus

so that we might buttress one another
against this world's stuffy opprobrium.

Even when

I die, I will still exist, for my body
will exist, will it not, and be just as
present in the world as any piece

of furniture or child's toy or fallen leaf
that lifts a little in a breeze.
And even when I'm simplified to bone

or ash, then that ash or bone will still
be *of* myself, containing, as it shall,
my distinctive molecules, which,

having dwelt in me for my life's span,
will retain a vestige of my scent on them,
and whose electrons must forever spin

with that particular character
they once expressed in the way I ran
for a bus or caught the barman's eye.

How pure I feel, now I am this ash
I rub between my fingers.
I'm wearing the black tie and white shirt,

and the pale grey suit which ash always
wears. Too pale, perhaps,
for a funeral. What do you think?

Trees, Breeze and Rabbits

Trees are made out of wood in
a deplorable waste

of a scarce resource that could have
been used to fashion cots for orphans,

or wooden legs for victims
of industrial accidents.

Just look at those nasty trees flaunt
their leaves, each one a tra-la-la.

Suck it up! say the trees,
and the giggling breeze wantons

in their leaves.
What a horrid nincompoop,

what a waste of space the breeze
is, with its heartlessness

and its insubstantiality!
And the rabbits, each, in itself,

just a small portion of meat,
but add them all up, add up all

the world's rabbits, and then
they're one enormous bunny.

A behemothic rodent which could
mindlessly hop on top of my house

and crush my wife and children
as well as myself as I attempt

to rescue them. I hate you all,
trees, breeze, and most of all, rabbits.

Childhood

But it is surely one of
the warmest territories,
with the muted chin-music
and the slippery houses
which, loosening their
loveliness, slide slowly
down the hill to gather
in their uncertain clump
in the elfin park with
the stream running
shyly through it
like a skinny girl with her
heavy crocodile schoolbag
packed brim-full
with dithery cold water.
Hurry up little girl.
There is no tomorrow.